Table Of Contents

Guide To The Cover 6

Guide To The Eyes 7

What The Bible Teaches
About Life After Death 9

Purpose Of This Book 41

History Of Books Without Borders, His Story 43

About The Author 51

Guide Others To Heaven 53

Prayer To Receive Christ 55

Order Form 56

Lead Someone To Christ . . . . Inside Back Cover

Guide To The Cover

←Heaven

←Earth

←Outer Darkness (Great gulf)

←Hell

What The Bible Teaches About **Life** After **Death**

Dr. Carolyn Diemer

Books Without Borders
P.O. Box 15176
Lynchburg, Virginia 24502-9981

Published By:

Winters Publishing
P.O. Box 501
Greensburg, Indiana 47240
812-663-4948

© 2004 Carolyn Diemer

Printed in Korea

All rights reserved.

No part of this publication may be reproduced or transmitted
in any form or by any means without written permission of the
publisher except for brief excerpts by reviewers.

Scripture marked (KJV) taken from the King James Version.

Scripture marked (NKJV) taken from the New King James Version.
Copyright © 1982 by Thomas Nelson, Inc. Used by permission.
All rights reserved.

Library of Congress Control Number: 2004112614
ISBN 1-883651-23-9

Dedication

I dedicate this book to the people of all lands who want to know what happens to them after they die. God wants everyone to go to heaven. Read this book and learn His good plan
for you.

Guide To The Eyes

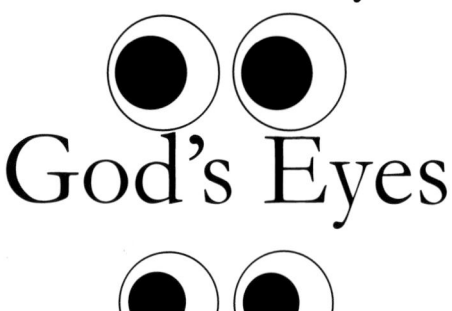

God's Eyes

The Devil's Eyes

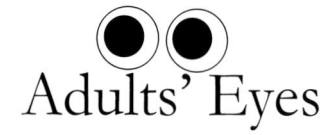

Adults' Eyes

Teenagers' Eyes

Children's Eyes

Babies' Eyes

Have you ever wondered what will happen to you after you die? The Bible, God's Word, teaches us that there are two possible places we can go: heaven or hell. God has a good plan for everyone to go to heaven. Read this book and find out how you can go to heaven.

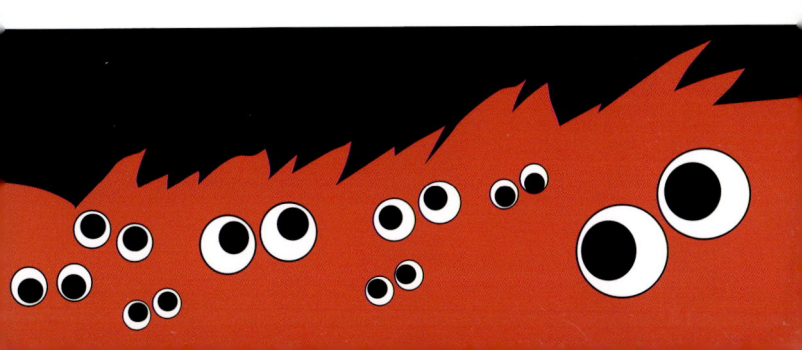

Hell is a real place.

"... the rich man also died and was buried; ... and in hell he lift up his eyes."
    Luke 16:22b, 23a (KJV)

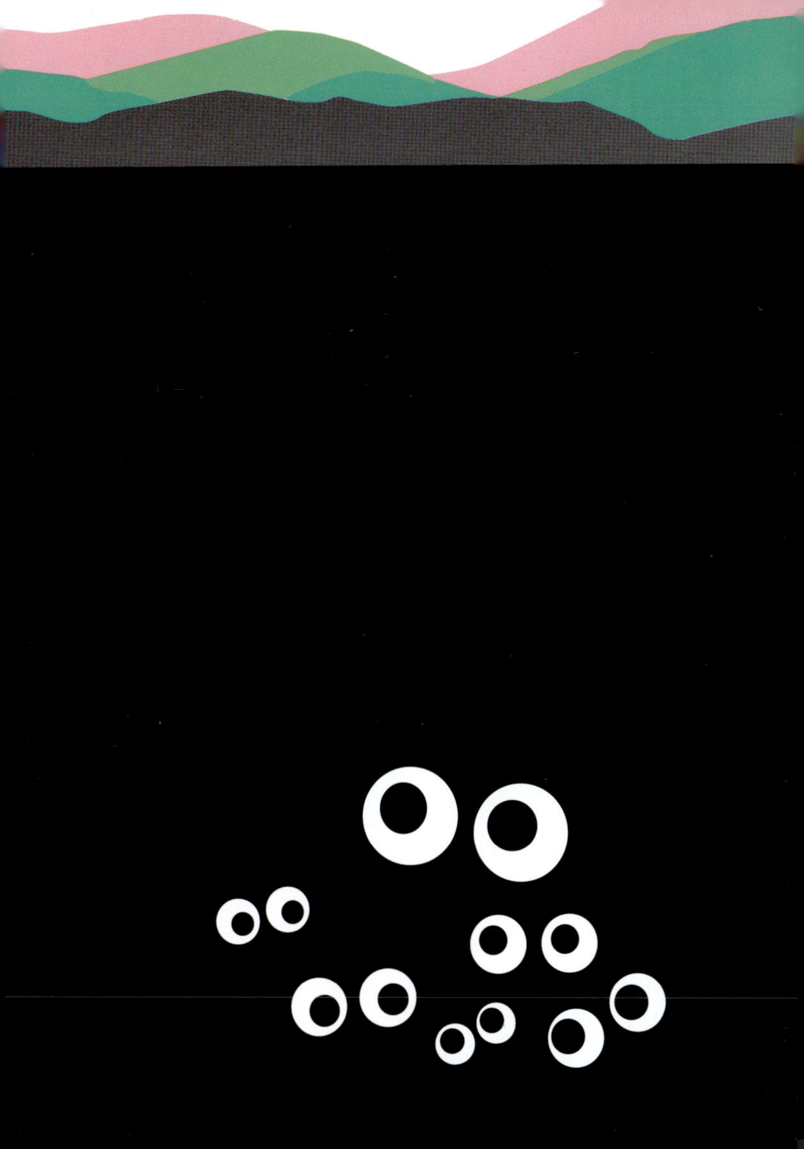

Hell was made by God for the devil and his angels.

"Then shall He say also unto them on the left hand, depart from me, ye cursed, into everlasting fire, prepared for the devil and his angels:"
Matthew 25:41 (KJV)

Hell is a lake of fire.

"And the devil that deceived them was cast into the lake of fire and brimstone,..."
Revelation 20:10a (KJV)

God does not want anyone to go to hell.

"Even so it is not the will of your Father which is in heaven, that one of these little ones should perish."

Matthew 18:14 (KJV)

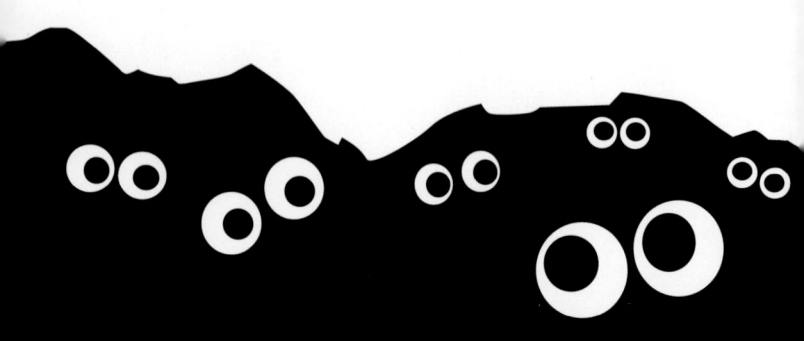

Hell is a place of outer darkness.

"And cast ye the unprofitable servant into outer darkness..."
Matthew 25:30a (KJV)

There are people in hell. They are men, women, and young people who died and never received Jesus as their Savior.

"In flaming fire taking vengeance on them that know not God, and that obey not the gospel of our Lord Jesus Christ:...."
　　　　II Thessalonians 1:8 (KJV)

People who go to hell cannot get out.

"And besides all this, between us and you there is a great gulf fixed, so that those who want to pass from here to you cannot, nor can those from there pass to us."
Luke 16:26 (NKJV)

People who go to hell have to stay forever.

"These shall be punished with everlasting destruction from the presence of the Lord and from the glory of His power,"
    II Thessalonians 1:9 (NKJV)

People who are in hell do not want other people to come there.

"Then he said, 'I beg you therefore, father, that you would send him to my father's house, for I have five brothers, that he may testify to them, lest they also come to this place of torment.'"
Luke 16:27, 28 (NKJV)

You cannot be good enough to stay out of hell; even some angels are in hell.

"For by grace are ye saved through faith; and that not of yourselves: it is the gift of God: Not of works, lest any man should boast."
Ephesians 2:8, 9 (KJV)

"God spared not the angels that sinned, but cast them down to hell..."
II Peter 2:4a (KJV)

God loved us so much that He made a way for us to stay out of hell.

"For God so loved the world, that he gave his only begotten Son that whosoever believeth in him should not perish, but have everlasting life."
John 3:16 (KJV)

God sent Jesus, His only Son, to the world to die for our sins so we could be saved from hell.

"...Christ died for our sins according to the scriptures;"
I Corinthians 15:3b (KJV)

Jesus died on the cross so He could forgive all our sins and no one would have to go to hell. He did not stay dead. He came back to life.

"...Christ died for our sins according to the scriptures; and that he was buried, and that he rose again the third day according to the scriptures:"

I Corinthians 15:3b, 4 (KJV)

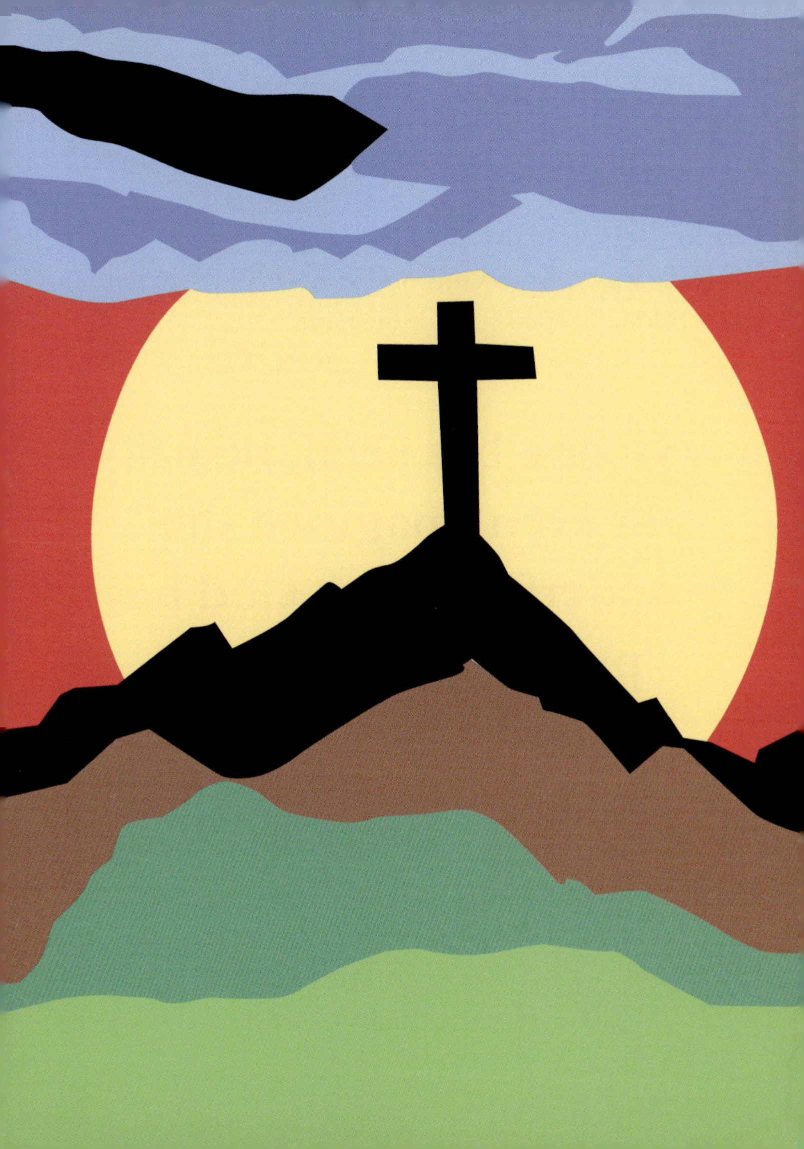

Heaven is a real place.
It is a beautiful city.

"And I John saw the Holy City, new Jerusalem, coming down from God out of heaven, prepared as a bride adorned for her husband."

Revelation 21:2 (KJV)

No one has seen, heard, or even imagined the wonderful things God has prepared for people who love Him.

"But as it is written, EYE HATH NOT SEEN, NOR EAR HEARD, NEITHER HAVE ENTERED INTO THE HEART OF MAN, THE THINGS WHICH GOD HATH PREPARED FOR THEM THAT LOVE HIM."

I Corinthians 2:9 (KJV)

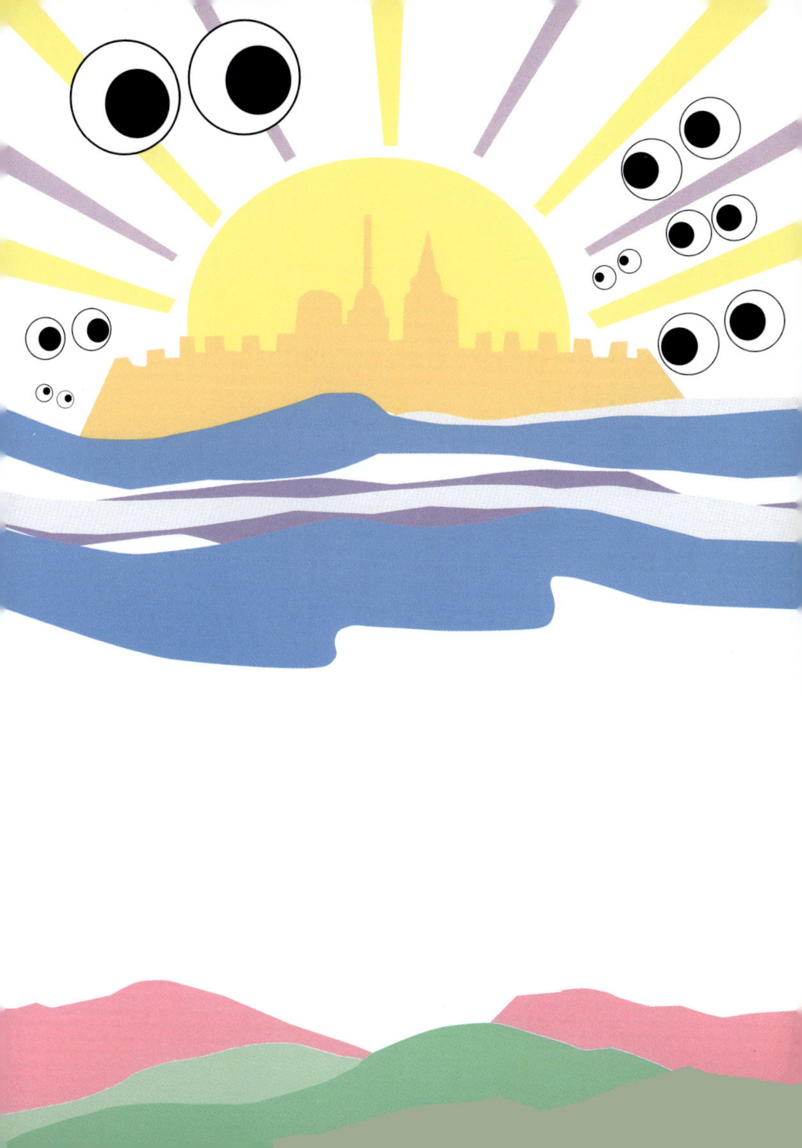

We see and understand only a little about God now, but when we get to heaven we will see Him face to face in His completeness.

"For now we see in a mirror, dimly, but then face to face..."
I Corinthians 13:12a (NKJV)

Heaven is a place of learning. I will understand everything clearly, just like God sees into my heart now.

"...Now I know in part, but then I shall know just as I also am known."
I Corinthians 13:12b (NKJV)

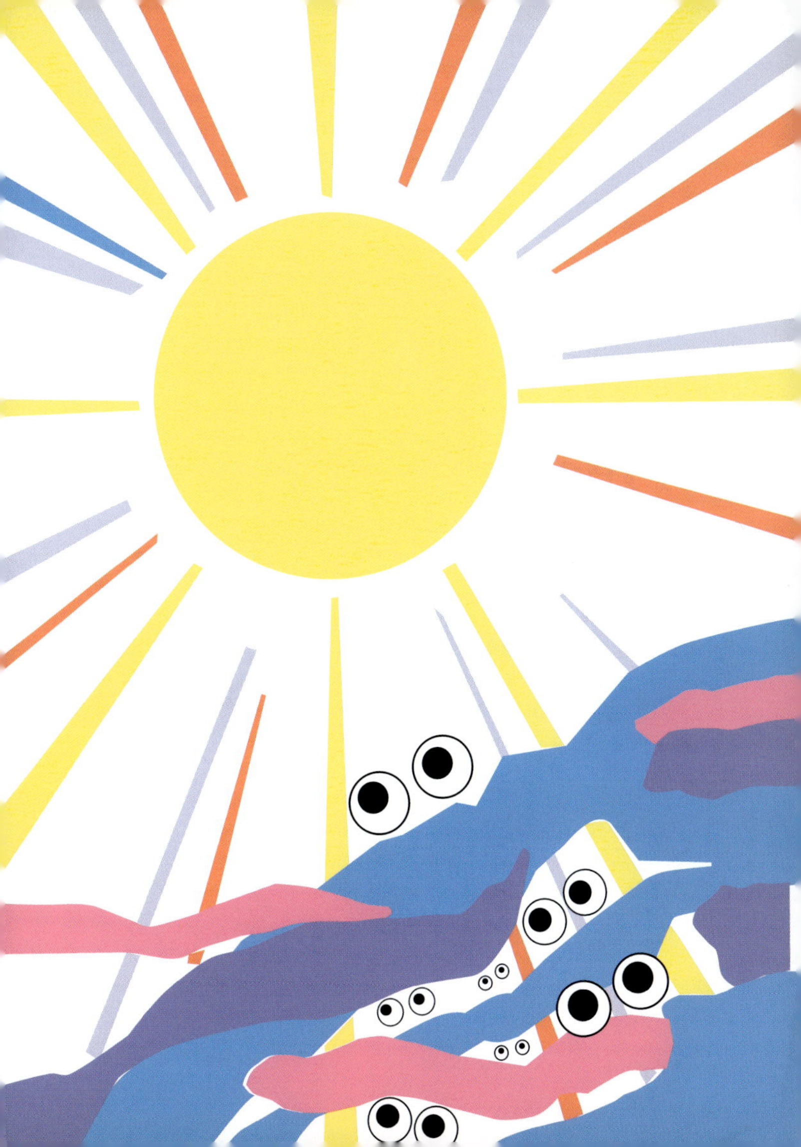

Heaven's walls are thick and high. Angels guard the twelve gates.

"And had a wall great and high, and had twelve gates, and at the gates twelve angels,…"
                    Revelation 21:12a (KJV)

Heaven's gates are made of pearl. The main street of the city is pure transparent gold.

"The twelve gates were twelve pearls: each individual gate was of one pearl. And the street of the city was pure gold, like transparent glass."
Revelation 21:21 (NKJV)

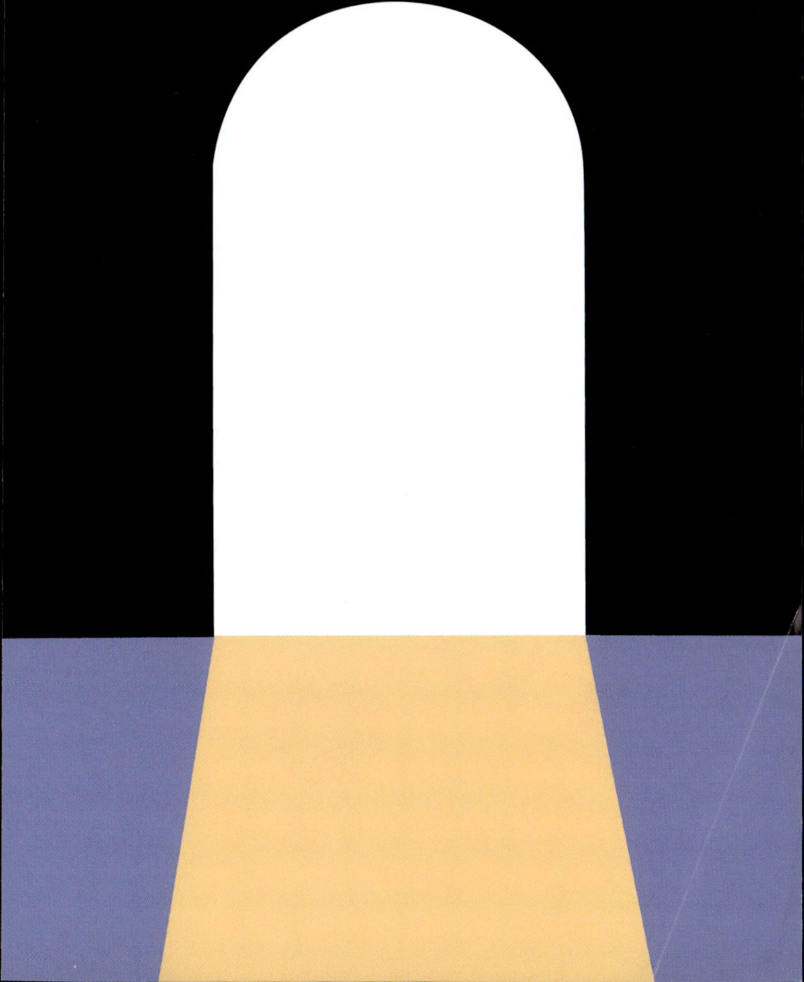

Heaven's foundations are made of beautiful stones.

Jasper

Sapphire

Chalcedony

Emerald

Sardonyx

Sardius

Chrysolite

Beryl

Topaz

Chrysoprase

Jacinth

Amethyst

"The foundations of the wall of the city were adorned with all kinds of precious stones:..."

Revelation 21:19a (NKJV)

Heaven is full of light and has no need of the sun or moon. The glory of God and Jesus will illuminate it. Heaven's light is for all the world.

"The city had no need of the sun or of the moon to shine in it, for the glory of God illuminated it. The Lamb is its light. And the nations of those who are saved shall walk in its light, and the kings of the earth bring their glory and honor into it."
Revelation 21:23, 24 (NKJV)

There is a beautiful river in heaven.

"And he showed me a pure river of water of life, clear as crystal, proceeding from the throne of God and of the Lamb."
Revelation 22:1 (NKJV)

There are trees of life in heaven. The leaves are used to heal all nations.

"In the middle of its street, and on either side of the river, was the tree of life, which bore twelve fruits, each tree yielding its fruit every month. The leaves of the tree were for the healing of the nations."
Revelation 22:2 (NKJV)

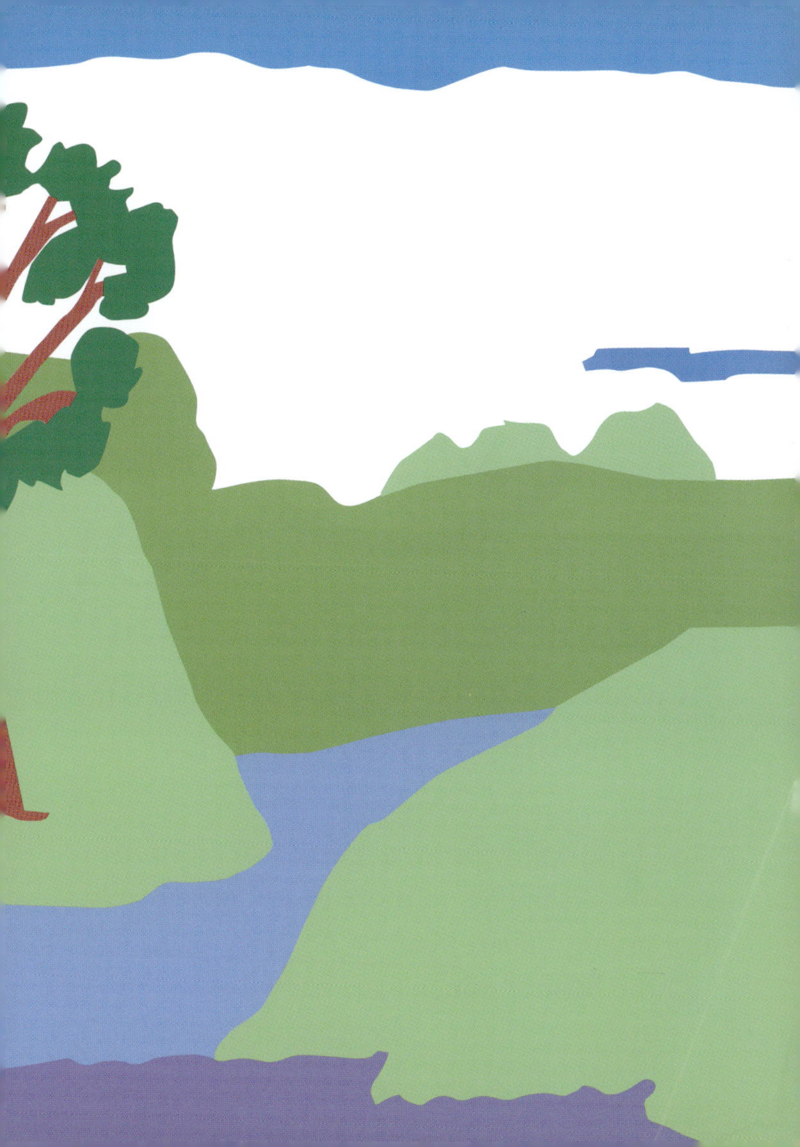

NO!

God will wipe away all tears in heaven. There will be no death, crying, or pain forever.

"And God will wipe away every tear from their eyes; there shall be no more death, nor sorrow, nor crying. There shall be no more pain, for the former things have passed away."
Revelation 21:4 (NKJV)

Heaven is a place of singing by people from all nations and all languages.

"And they sang a new song, saying, Thou are worthy to take the book and to open the seals thereof: for thou wast slain, and has redeemed us to God by thy blood out of every kindred, and tongue, and people, and nation;"
Revelation 5:9 (KJV)

THE BOOK OF LIFE

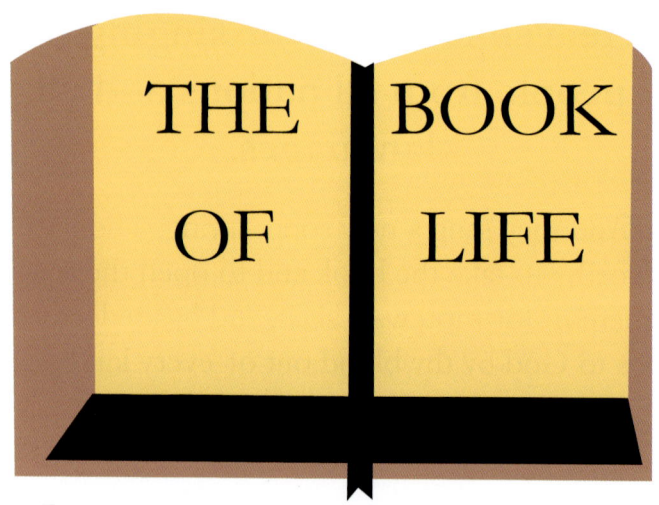

Do you want your name in the Lamb's Book of Life?

No sin is in heaven and only a person whose name is written in the Lamb's Book of Life will be there.

"But there shall by no means enter it (*heaven*) anything that defiles, or causes an abomination or a lie, but only those who are written in the Lamb's Book of Life."

Revelation 21:27 (NKJV)

Prayer To Receive Christ

If you believe that God sent His Son Jesus, to die on the cross for your sins (the bad things you have done against God); that He was buried and rose again, and you are willing to ask Jesus to forgive (take away) your sins and come into your life, you can do that right now.

Pray (talk to God): (1) confess (agree with God) that you are a sinner; (2) tell God some of the sinful things you have done; (3) ask Jesus to forgive all your sins of lying, stealing, cheating, disobeying your parents, or other sins He brings to your mind; (4) ask Jesus to come into your life; (5) ask Jesus to accept you into God's family and direct your life. Believe in Him, as your Lord and Savior.

If you have prayed this prayer sincerely, you do not need to be afraid that you will go to hell when you die. You are now a Christian (a believer in Jesus Christ), and when you die, you will go to heaven and you will be there with God forever.

It is not important where you are and when you say this prayer. It is important that you talked to God, that He heard you, forgave your sins and that you are accepted into His family. And if you believe in Christ sincerely, you have the full right to call yourself a CHRISTIAN.

The Purpose Of The English Version Of This Book

Over 1,000,000 Russian copies of this book have now been printed and distributed throughout the former Soviet Union countries. The book has also been translated and is ready for printing in Hindi, standard Spanish, Arabic, and Turkish. The profits from the sale of the English version will be used to print additional copies for free distribution around the world.

For additional information about Books Without Borders or to make a donation to help spread the Word, please contact:

Carolyn Diemer
Books Without Borders
P.O. Box 15176
Lynchburg, VA 24502-9981

Look at:
www.bookswithoutborders.net

History of Books Without Borders, His Story

"According as he hath chosen us in him before the foundation of the world,…"   *Ephesians 1:4a* (KJV)

God had a plan! Before the world began, God had a plan for the whole world to be saved through Jesus' death on the cross. At the age of ten, I accepted God's plan and asked Jesus to save me. At fourteen, I publicly acknowledged that God had called me to full-time Christian service. I yielded my life to the Lord to go anywhere and do anything He wanted me to do. In 1993, at age fifty-five, I asked God to help me share the Gospel with people around the world in a unique way. Two years later He enabled me to step out on faith in Him to write and illustrate *What The Bible Teaches About Life After Death,* in such a clear and simple way that it can be translated into any language.

God overwhelmed me in 1995 when a family, who wishes to remain anonymous, gave $100,000 to finance translating the book into Russian, printing, and distributing the book into former Soviet Union countries.

In 1995, the anonymous donors requested that I start a non-profit organization. As a result, on July 7, 1995,

Books Without Borders was created. This name was chosen because the long term goal of Books Without Borders is to transcend all borders around the world and communicate the Gospel to all people in every country. This organization was founded and continues to operate on the command of Jesus - The Great Commission - "Go ye into all the world, and preach the Gospel…" Mark 16:15a (KJV).

At this writing, over one million dollars has been given by many people across America to begin to accomplish this goal. In addition to being translated into Russian, *What The Bible Teaches About Life After Death* has now been translated into standard Spanish, Hindi, Arabic, and Turkish; it is now ready to be printed and distributed to many more parts of the world.

Books Without Borders History, His (God's) Story

Over the years God has heavily burdened my heart for people all over the world to become believers in the only Savior of the world, Jesus Christ. Each year since 1996, He has continued to make ways for this to become a reality.

At the University of Virginia, I took a graduate children's literature course. God used an inspiring professor to motivate me to not only write a book for class credit, but also later to write *What The Bible Teaches About Life After Death*. The principles learned in that class enabled me to write and illustrate this book in such a way that it can have a global effect. The eye illustrations are generic, the pictures of heaven and hell are symbolic, and the biblical concepts included will stand forever.

In February of 1996, the first Books Without Borders newsletter, "Books Without Borders News," was mailed to many churches and Christian friends. Recipients generously responded with gifts totaling over $150,000.

In June of 1996, thousands of books were distributed in Russia for the first time. My husband and I also traveled to Minsk, Belarus where *What The Bible Teaches About Life After Death* is printed. While there we heard Russian General Vycheslav Borisov's personal testimony of how he cried out to be saved when the helicopter he was in was shot down during the Russian war with Afghanistan.

Later that year, upon his visit to America, we met General Borisov and he asked to see a copy of *What The Bible Teaches About Life After Death*. He read the book and stated, "I want a copy of this book for every Russian soldier!" Not knowing how many Russian troops there were, I just started asking God to provide the funds. Then the gifts started to come. First a $70,000 gift came, then a $40,000 gift, a $30,000 gift, and many more smaller, yet important, gifts.

In 1997, people across America responded to a letter to get *What the Bible Teaches About Life After Death* to the Russian people by giving $116,000. Through Revival Fires Ministries, headed by Rev. Cecil Todd, I met his son, Chuck, and daughter-in-law, Helen, who is Russian born. Through them God enabled us to meet the head of 70,000 Russian public schools while at the Russian Federation of Education in Moscow. While in Moscow we were able to share the gospel in the classrooms through *What the Bible Teaches About Life After Death* and distribute 5,000 copies to students and faculty.

As copies of *What The Bible Teaches About Life After Death* were discovered by missionaries throughout former Soviet Union countries, they began to regularly request copies of this book for distribution. Josh McDowell Ministries and The Samaritan's Purse representatives each requested 40,000 copies. Ten thousand copies were requested for Ukraine. Five thousand copies were given to the Association of Christian Schools International where members of Calvary Church in Moscow agreed to distribute the book. Advancing Native Missions enabled Books Without Borders to get 5,000 copies of *What The Bible Teaches About Life After Death* to a pastors' conference in Siberia. Through a single mom at my church, God miraculously provided the needed $500 to airlift these books from World Wide Printing in Minsk, Belarus to Siberia.

During the summer of 1997, we met General Borisov in Moscow and delivered thousands of copies of *What The Bible Teaches About Life After Death* to an army base outside Moscow.

A Books Without Borders group of nine traveled to Kiev, Ukraine during the summer of 1998. Upon our arrival we discovered that the books were sealed in a room, and we could not distribute them without paying an import tax. Not wanting to set a precedent for future trips to the Ukraine, we refused to pay the import tax. After we left the country and the government officials were sure that the books were not to be sold, but were indeed a gift, they allowed the Ukrainian churches to distribute the books. Forty-thousand books were distributed throughout Ukraine, which has a population of approximately fifty-three million.

In June of 1999, our group of eleven went to Moldova, a small inland former Soviet Union country. We experienced great religious freedom. In two large cities, the city band played Christian songs while seated on the porch of a five-hundred seat Cultural Center. In the past, these buildings where we met for evangelistic services had actually served as Communist Headquarters Training Centers. We helped distribute 10,000 copies of this book to the people of Moldova, on street corners, in schools, and orphanages.

In June of 2000, the Books Without Borders mission team of twelve ministered in Pushino and Seplakov, cities outside Moscow. This group helped to deliver 50,000 books to the Russian military, orphans, drug rehab patients, juvenile delinquent girls, elderly ladies, hospital patients, guests in our hotel, people on the street, firemen, and to a large crowd at a Saturday flea market.

On July 12, 2001, our group, along with many other Christians from across America, boarded a large boat in Moscow. We traveled to six cities along the Volga River. The entire group handed out 50,000 New Testaments and 10,000 copies of *What The Bible Teaches About Life After Death*.

In July, 2002, the Books Without Borders missions team raised $15,000 for Bibles to present to people along with a copy of *What The Bible Teaches About Life After Death*. While in Russia, various members of our team of fifteen preached, gave testimonies, presented the "Our Redeemer" pantomime, conducted Open Air Evangelistic Campaigns through street art, and sang in six cities along the Volga River. This team also ministered to people in orphanages, hospitals, at bus stops, train stations, flea markets, and in churches.

In July, 2003, the mission team members traveled

to Saint Petersburg, Russia, where the Diemers led a conference for Russian Pastors and Russian Ladies for the city of St. Petersburg. There we also ministered to people at an orphanage, refugee camp, young men's drug rehabilitation center, and a youth camp. We also handed out copies of the book to people at a train station and to a large crowd at a market place.

Between 1996 and 2004, the generous giving of Christian friends across America provided funds for over one million Russian copies to be distributed in many former Soviet Union countries. Since the book has now been translated into Hindi, standard Spanish, Arabic, and Turkish, the doors are wide open to continue to spread the gospel around the world through *What The Bible Teaches About Life After Death*.

God's plan continued to grow when Books Without Borders received an anonymous $25,000 gift to have *What The Bible Teaches About Life After Death* published in English. All profits from the sale of this book will be used to print the book in other languages. Jesus' command still stands, "Go ye into all the world, and preach the gospel..." Mark 16:15 (KJV).

You are an important part of God's plan. As we thank God for all the people who have taught us and stand with us, let us now invest in the lives of others in our family, those in our neighborhood, and people around the world. It is still God's plan, and it is a perfect plan, to reach the world that includes you. You are important to God!

"According as he hath chosen us in him before the foundation of the world,…"   *Ephesians 1:4a (KJV)*

"Go ye into all the world, and preach the gospel to every creature..."   *Mark 16:15 (KJV)*

"The Lord is ... not willing that any should perish, but that all should come to repentance."   *II Peter 3:9b (KJV)*

His plan is perfect!

About The Author

Carolyn Sparks Diemer was born in Bakersville, North Carolina. Her parents took her to church regularly. At age ten, Carolyn asked Jesus Christ to forgive all her sins and she was born again. At age fourteen, she publicly yielded her life to full-time Christian service.

Carolyn received the following degrees: A.A., Gardner-Webb College; B.S. in Elementary Education, Carson-Newman College; M.R.E., Southwestern Seminary. Dr. Diemer received the Ed.D. from Nova University. She served as a professor of education in Liberty University's School of Education for twenty-seven years and part-time in Liberty Baptist Theological Seminary.

Dr. Diemer retired from Liberty University in 2001, and now serves as a pastor's wife and President of Books Without Borders. She is married to Dr. Carl John Diemer, who is Professor of Church History at Liberty Baptist Theological Seminary, the school he helped to establish in 1973. Dr. Carl Diemer also serves as Pastor of Leesville Road Baptist Church, Evington, Virginia. Her husband Carl's love and support have provided a firm foundation which continues to help build Books Without Borders. They have one daughter, Christy, and one son, Curt, who is married to Tammy Thomas.

The Diemers have four delightful grandchildren, James, Anna, Amber, and Alise.

Out of a rich and varied background of teaching over 5,000 Liberty University students from around the world and traveling to fourteen countries, Carolyn has observed that children, young people, and adults are curious and have many questions about what will happen to them after they die. This book has been written to inform individuals of the facts that the Bible, God's Word, teaches about life after death.

If you would like to write to Dr. Carolyn Diemer, her address is Books Without Borders, P. O. Box 15176, Lynchburg, VA 24502-9981.

Visit the website:
www.bookswithoutborders.net

Now That You Are a Believer in Jesus, Use This Guide to Help Others Go to Heaven When They Die.

1) Say, "Have you ever wondered what will happen to you when you die?"

2) Ask "What do you think will happen to you when you die? Why do you think this?"

3) Say, "I would like to tell you what the Bible teaches about life after death."

4) Turn to the picture of the cross on Page 23. Say, "The Bible tells us that Jesus died on the cross for our sins." Repeat John 3:16 (KJV), "For God so loved the world, that he gave his only begotten Son, that whosoever believeth in him should not perish, but have everlasting life." Repeat Romans 3:23 (KJV). "For all have sinned, and come short of the glory of God."

5) Say, "Do you believe Jesus died on the cross? Do you believe you have sinned? Do you believe Jesus died for your sins?" Repeat Romans 5:8 (KJV), "But God commendeth his love toward us, in that, while we were yet sinners, Christ died for us." Give your own personal testimony of how God saved you. No matter what the response is, go to Step 6.

6) Say, "Would you like to talk to God and ask Him to forgive (take away) your sins?" If the answer is yes -

7) Say, "Repeat this prayer after me." (Use the prayer on the following page.) If they say, "No," remind them that Jesus said in John 14:6 (KJV), "... I am the way, the truth, and the life: and no man cometh unto the Father, but by me."

Prayer to Receive Christ as Your Savior:

Dear Jesus, (1) I believe you died on the cross for my sins, that you were buried and that you arose from the dead. (2) I agree with you that I am a sinner. (3) I have done things against you that displease you (tell Jesus some of the sinful things you have done). (4) Jesus, I ask you to forgive all my sins of lying, cheating, stealing, disobeying people in authority, other sins you bring to my mind, and other sins that I do not remember. (5) Jesus, I ask you to accept me into God's family, and direct my life and take me to heaven when I die. Amen.

Now that you are a believer in Jesus, you will want to lead others to Christ. Use the guide on the inside back cover to help you lead people to Christ. Then they will also go to heaven when they die.

Tell them God will be pleased when they tell others what God has just done in their life. Encourage them to give or mail this book to the person(s) God brought to their mind.

Order Form
What The Bible Teaches About Life After Death

If you would like to order additional copies of *What The Bible Teaches About Life After Death*, please feel free to copy this page and return to:

Winters Publishing
P.O. Box 501
Greensburg, IN 47240

Please send me:

_____ copies at $5.95 each $ _____

Shipping: $2.00 1st book,
$1.00 each additional $ _____

IN residents: 6% sales tax $ _____

TOTAL $ _____

Send to:

Name: _____

Address: _____

City: _____ State: ____ Zip: _____